Missing
Butterfly
Feelings

Nan Nelson, MD
Child Phychiatrist

*To Violet, Margot, Mom + Dad
I am sorry for your loss. I hope
this helps.
Nan Nelson
12/14/2022*

Dedication: The little girl in Hospice who heard this story first.

In my third year of medical school, I was asked to go see a 2 year old girl with a brain tumor that was having a hard time understanding what was happening to her. I used pictures from books to tell this story. It was also of use for her brothers, sisters, and parents.

Notes to Parents and Guardians of Children

Most adults don't know how to talk about death, let alone explain it to children. Sometimes I tell adults this story and invite them to use it as a tool for communication. It helps to have tools to use each time a death occurs in the circle of life, whether it is human or the death of a beloved pet.

Young children think concretely. For example: if you give them two glasses of water, one tall and thin and one short and fat, and ask which has the most liquid, they will choose the tall one every time, even if you show them that you are adding a half a cup to each glass. They will often tell you the moon is following them, or that the wind is talking to them. Abstract thinking does not come along until early adolescence (about 10 to 13 years of age). This is when children can begin to understand death and dying. Young children will not understand that "someone has died and gone to Heaven." When they see someone "die" on television, and then see that same actor on a different show - do you see how that would confuse them? It's because of the ability to think in the abstract.

Often families say that they have given a complete explanation of the death process to the child, only to have them come back later with questions like, "When does Grandpa come home from work?" or other questions. This is how a child processes ideas. Adults do too - it just looks different. Just as adults will distract themselves with mindless tasks such as cleaning, children will often play to help them make sense of what they've been told.

Families often ask if children should go to a funeral, or view a person in a casket. Funerals, wakes, visitation, and graveside ceremonies are all ways for us to process, honor, and say goodbye. To some degree, the children will follow your lead. However, do not expect them to sit like an adult through the process. You may want to hire a babysitter or brings toys or books with you to distract them. Parents often worry that they are traumatizing the child by attending ceremonies, or visiting sick loved ones in hospitals. However, the death and dying process is important for young and old alike. Saying goodbye is important for everyone.

This book is about allowing you to communicate about what has transpired. You may have to read this book more than once with your child. You may want to get caterpillars and release butterflies. Libraries have wonderful books about butterflies. You can use life experiences to address the concept of death in everyday life. For example: some of the first conversations with my children began with earthworms that had died on the sidewalk.

Usually the first year is the hardest, especially around holidays. Go at your own pace. These communication skills will allow you to talk with your child as they grow and develop. Making new memories makes it easier, and can also be a way to remember loved ones. One woman bought a new Christmas tree ornament each year for her baby that died to help the family remember.

Remember, this is a process. Be gentle with yourselves and your children. Follow normal routines. May you find peace in this difficult time.

Nan Nelson
Child Psychiatrist

Humans are like caterpillars.

They pop out of their eggs wherever their eggs are laid.

They don't get to choose where that happens.

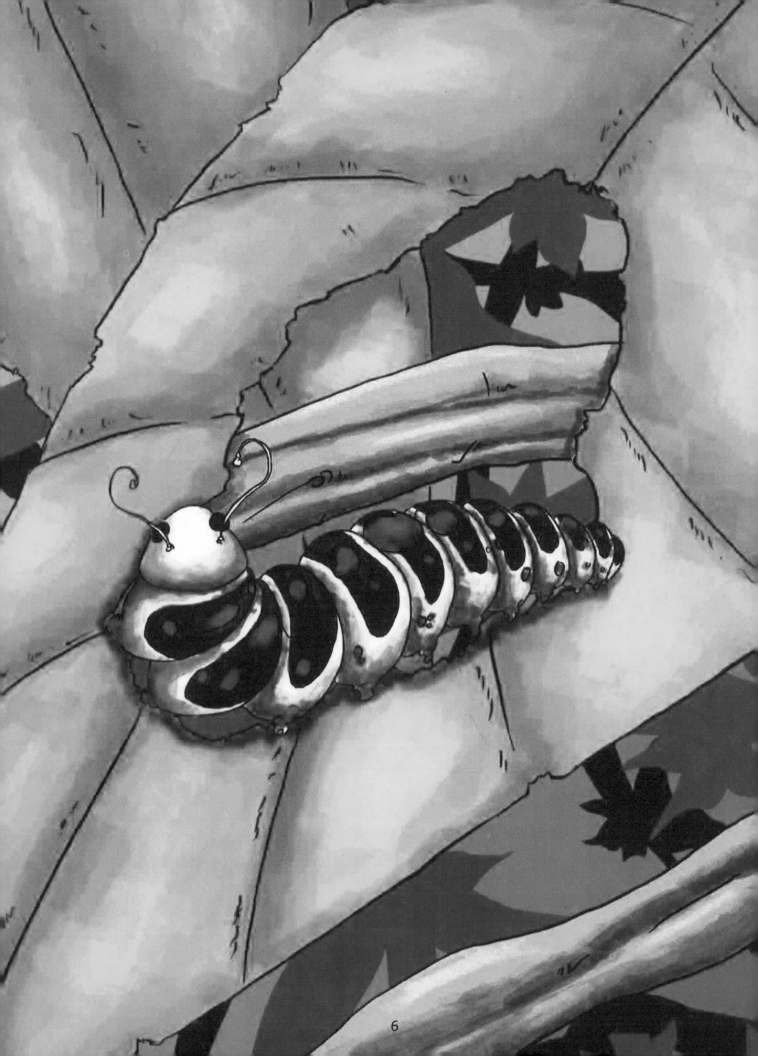

The Caterpillar crawls out,
It eats,
It sleeps,
and it poops when it needs to.
Just like you.

Caterpillars may even go to school.
Some children don't believe that they do,
but how do caterpillars know what to eat
if they get blown off the leaf and need to keep eating?
Or their brother or sister knocks them off the leaf?
Or how to hide under the leaf if it's raining?

Eventually some caterpillars lay eggs
and some don't.
Just like some humans have children
and some don't.

Then an amazing thing happens.

The Caterpillar begins to spin a cocoon.

Some caterpillars build their cocoons very fast,
some build it very slow.

Some cocoons are messy,

Some are very neat and tidy.

It's not something caterpillars have control over.

It just happens.

What happens when the Caterpillar builds a cocoon?
On the outside it doesn't look like much is happening.
On the inside something called metamorphosis has
happened.
Metamorphosis is the big word
for the amazing change of becoming a butterfly.
When the Caterpillar is ready,
it splits open the cocoon and out comes a butterfly.

When the butterfly first comes out, it's still wet, and has to flap its wings to dry them out. Then the butterfly rests for a few minutes because it takes a lot of work to come out of the cocoon and dry off.

When the butterfly is ready, it can fly away.
It's free.
Does it go back into the cocoon?
It would not really fit very well.
Can it come back and visit the cocoon?
It could.

What happens to the cocoon after
the butterfly flies away?
Well, it's just a papery shell that
falls apart pretty easily.
Does the butterfly need the cocoon anymore?
Nope.

22

By now you have figured out

that this is what happens to humans when they die.

Their body builds a cocoon,

so some people are sick for a short time and then die,

some people are sick for a long time before they die.

And sometimes it happens in a blink of an eye.

It's not something you or the person has control over.

When a human becomes a butterfly,

do they need their body anymore?

No. The reason they bury it is because it would stink.

Does the cocoon go to the bathroom?

Does it sleep?

Does it eat?

No, doesn't need to.

Just like the butterfly, the human spirit or soul is free.

Sometimes after someone dies,
people see or hear the person that has
become a butterfly.
That's really common.
It doesn't mean that something bad is happening.
It's no different than the butterfly
coming back to visit the other caterpillars.

Now that you know what happens,
when you see something that reminds you
of the person who died,
you can talk about missing caterpillar feelings,
missing cocoon feelings,
or missing butterfly feelings.

It's normal to have feelings about people
or animals when they die.
It's like going to the beach or a big lake
where the waves crash over you.
At first the waves may feel like they're crashing
again and again and again,
and you almost can't catch your breath.

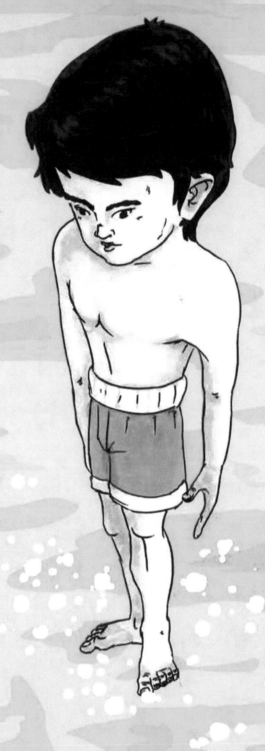

Then there's sometimes a break in the waves.
Sometimes children feel bad, like how come
I don't feel sad anymore?
But soon another big wave comes.
Sometimes these waves happen in places
that you don't think they will,
Like the grocery store,
the playground,
the library,
or someplace that reminds you of the person
that's now a butterfly.
That's normal.
You may even feel like you're going to cry,
or that you have an ache in your chest.
It's okay.
Eventually it will begin to get better.

You may even get to the point when you
see the wave coming.
You bend your knees.
Maybe you even pick up your feet as the
wave comes towards you,
floating through the crash.
Then putting down your feet,
and it doesn't knock you over like it did
in the beginning.

After a person becomes a butterfly,

it takes time to get used to that person not being around.

It's ok to have these feelings.

Every child does this at their own pace,

some faster or

some slower than others.

Take your time. It may take time for the grownups

around you to go through this too.

May you find peace as you go through this loss.

The End
&
the Beginning in the Circle of Life and Death

CPSIA information can be obtained
at www.ICGtesting.com
Printed in the USA
BVHW020028061122
651013BV00002B/4